the guide to owning a
Basset Hound

Lisa Puskas

Photo: Isabelle Francais

D1609490

© T.F.H. Publications, Inc.

Distributed in the UNITED STATES to the Pet Trade by T.F.H. Publications, Inc., 1 TFH Plaza, Neptune City, NJ 07753; on the Internet at www.tfh.com; in CANADA by Rolf C. Hagen Inc., 3225 Sartelon St., Montreal, Quebec H4R 1E8; Pet Trade by H & L Pet Supplies Inc., 27 Kingston Crescent, Kitchener, Ontario N2B 2T6; in ENGLAND by T.F.H. Publications, PO Box 74, Havant PO9 5TT; in AUSTRALIA AND THE SOUTH PACIFIC by T.F.H. (Australia), Pty. Ltd., Box 149, Brookvale 2100 N.S.W., Australia; in NEW ZEALAND by Brooklands Aquarium Ltd., 5 McGiven Drive, New Plymouth, RD1 New Zealand; in SOUTH AFRICA by Rolf C. Hagen S.A. (PTY.) LTD., P.O. Box 201199, Durban North 4016, South Africa; in Japan by T.F.H. Publications. Published by T.F.H. Publications, Inc.

MANUFACTURED IN THE
UNITED STATES OF AMERICA
BY T.F.H. PUBLICATIONS, INC.

Contents

The Publisher wishes to acknowledge the following owners of the dogs in this book, including: Rene Bendsten, Kathleen Blake, Anne-Terese Borck, Jim and Evaline Dow, Marit Jenssen, Kathy Kastner, Claudia Lane, Vickie McMackin, Baba Monk, Jerry and Carol O'Bryant, Jennifer Parish, Brian and Janice Pechtold, Pamela Robbins, Mary Smizer, Penny Swan, Dawn Towne, Nancy Willis.

Photo: Isabelle Francais

History of the Basset Hound

The Basset Hound is well-known for his keen sense of smell and tracking ability; however, he is also a highly intelligent, savvy hunter that can outsmart a rabbit that might have leapt over brush or across a road leaving little scent. Over the years, several breeds were interbred to produce a hound with a perfect blend of the qualities that early Basset Hound breeders were looking for.

FRENCH ORIGINS

The St. Hubert hounds were a popular French hunting hound in 700 AD. Over several hundred years, this hound was crossed with other hounds to produce many distinct breeds. Two of these breeds were the Basset Normand and the Basset Artois. They were crossed to produce the Basset Artesien Normand, which became a popular hunting and show dog in France. These hounds were considerably different from the present-day Basset Hound: taller and lighter boned, with tighter skin, and of considerably less weight. These keen-nosed scenthounds, so called because they hunted primarily by scent, were used to slowly and steadily trail rabbits and game birds. Stamina, rather than speed,

Driven by their keen sense of smell, Bassets are well known for their excellent tracking and hunting abilities. Alcapone, owned by Rene Bendsten and Ann-Therese Bork, and Vahhala's Wilda Finn, owned by Marit Jenssen.
Photo: Marit Jenssen

The word "Basset" means low set in French. Over the years, several breeds were crossed to produce a hound with the perfect blend of qualities that is useful for the field. *Photo: Isabelle Francais*

GUIDE TO OWNING A BASSET HOUND

was the key element in this form of hunting. The word "basset" means low set in French.

ENGLISH INFLUENCE

In the 1870s, Englishmen Lord Onslow, George Krehl, and Everett Millais imported the Basset Artesien Normand from the well-known French show kennel of Count le Couteulx de Canteleu. One of Mr. Millais' imports was a hound named Model. His littermate, Fino de Paris, was imported by Mr. Krehl. Among Lord Onslow's imports was a hound named Fino. These hounds were heavily linebred and inbred, which became an important part of the foundation of the Basset Hound in England. Although they were excellent representatives of their breed at the time, they were quite different from present-day Basset Hounds in substance.

Many Bassets were imported to England from France; however, they were

Basset Hounds were bred to hunt in packs and work as a team. Ebba, Morgan, Soffi, and Sydney get ready for their midnight hunt. *Photo: Marit Jenssen*

all closely related. The small gene pool and constant inbreeding produced smaller and smaller hounds, along with many other problems. To help correct these problems, Bassets were imported from the heavier-boned, French Lane lines to cross with the English Bassets that descended from the Couteulx lines. These crosses did not completely solve the problems encountered by the breed. In 1892, Mr. Millais, in an effort to add more size and bone to the breed, crossed his Basset with a Bloodhound. This gave breeders what they were looking for—the heavy-boned, loose-skinned foundation stock of today's Basset Hound. The Bloodhound was again crossed with the Basset Hound in the 1930s to add more substance.

A Basset Hound club was formed in England in 1884. By the 1900s, the Basset Hound was regularly hunted in packs in England.

THROUGHOUT THE WORLD

Basset Hounds were imported to the US in the 1920s. These first hounds were imported from the English hunting packs for the purpose of hunting hare in the field. In 1935, the Basset Hound Club of America was formed. The breed became popular throughout Europe and is now found in most parts of the world.

Eight Basset Hound breed clubs are registered with The Kennel Club. Flat 3, 10 Boyne Park, Tunbridge Wells, Kent TN4 8ET England.

Characteristics of the Basset Hound

The Basset Hound is first and foremost a hunting hound. With his jovial attitude and calm disposition, it is sometimes easy to forget that today's Basset descends from some of Europe's finest hunting scenthounds. The Basset is a strong, athletic hound that can hunt over varied terrain. Every characteristic, from

The Basset is a strong, athletic hound with a low-set, powerful build. Bay Manor Majorette, owned by Jim and Evaline Dow, takes the ribbon. *Photo: Missy Yuhl*

The Basset's long, floppy ears are one of his most noticeable features. It is believed that the long ears help to capture the scent of game. *Photo: Vickie McMackin*

bone structure to temperament, was painstakingly bred into the Basset for a specific purpose.

DESCRIPTION OF BASSET HOUND FORM

Head

One of the most noticeable characteristics of the Basset's large head is the loose, wrinkly skin. This trait is highly desirable. The skin hangs in loose folds around the lips and down the front of the neck. It is important that the top of the skull has a rounded or domed appearance. The long muzzle appears to be strong. The ears are very long and set low and far back on the skull. It is believed that the loose skin and long ears help to capture the scent of game.

Neck

The head flows into a well-arched neck. Strong muscling should be evident in the Basset neck, because when he is tracking game, he holds his head close to the ground, moving it back and forth for long periods of time. The neck must be long enough to comfortably reach the ground.

Front

The Basset chest is deep and powerful and the breastbone is very prominent. The

The Basset should have a strong neck that is long enough to comfortably reach the ground, and he should be able to move with strength and ease in the field. *Photo: Jim Dow*

The Basset has a deep chest with a prominent breastbone. The legs are short, heavy, and strong, and turn outward to help him support the weight of his body. *Photo: Jim Dow*

The Basset's body needs to be strong and well muscled, with powerful hindquarters to provide forward momentum. *Photo: Sheela Cunningham*

front is well angled where the shoulder meets the upper arm. When the Basset is hunting with his head lowered, most of his weight is carried by the front legs. To carry this weight, the legs are well set under the body. The legs are short, heavy, and strong. Knuckling over (a forward bending of the wrist joint when standing)

would cause weakness in the front legs and is a disqualification.

The feet are large and have thick pads. They turn outward, which effectively helps the Basset to support and balance the heavy weight of his body.

Body and Hindquarters

The ribcage should appear rounded to allow for the great heart and lung capacity so necessary for stamina. The topline is strong, straight, and well muscled. The hindquarters must possess well-developed, rounded muscle, because it provides the Basset's forward momentum. A weak, poorly-built rear would not provide the needed propulsion and stamina.

Balanced Movement

Balance is the symmetry of a dog's separate parts in relationship to each other. The well-angulated rear balances the well-angulated front assembly. If any angle of the front or rear assembly were too straight, the dog would be out of balance and the result would be improper movement.

The Basset Hound should move easily with a smooth, coordinated gait. A poor-moving Basset could not efficiently cover ground while on the hunt. If you were to watch a Basset move in the sand, the tracks left by his right front and right rear feet would appear to follow each other in a straight line. Likewise with his left front and left rear feet. The Basset is built to gait with his nose close to the ground and cannot gait properly if his head is held high, as is sometimes done in the show ring.

A short-legged dog, the Basset Hound is heavier in bone, size considered, than any other breed of dog.

Photo: Isabelle Francais

Standard for the Basset Hound

AKC STANDARD FOR THE BASSET HOUND

General Appearance—The Basset Hound possesses in marked degree those characteristics which equip it admirably to follow a trail over and through difficult terrain. It is a short-legged dog, heavier in bone, size considered, than any other breed of dog, and while its movement is deliberate, it is in no sense clumsy. In temperament it is mild, never sharp or timid. It is capable of great endurance in the field and is extreme in its devotion.

Head—The head is large and well proportioned. Its length from occiput to muzzle is greater than the width at the brow. In overall appearance the head is of medium width. *The skull* is well domed, showing a pronounced occipital protuberance. A broad, flat skull is a fault. The length from nose to stop is approximately the length from stop to occiput. The sides are flat and free from cheek bumps. Viewed in profile, the top lines of the muzzle and skull are straight and lie in parallel planes, with a moderately defined stop. The skin over the whole of the head is loose, falling in distinct wrinkles over the brow when the

The Basset's head is large and well proportioned with soft eyes, a black nose with large, wide-open nostrils, and a heavy muzzle.
Photo: Marit Jennsen

head is lowered. A dry head and tight skin are faults. *The muzzle* is deep, heavy, and free from snipiness. *The nose* is darkly pigmented, preferably black, with large, wide-open nostrils. A deep liver-colored nose conforming to the coloring of the head is permissible, but not desirable. *The teeth* are large, sound, and regular, meeting in either a scissors or an even bite. A bite either overshot or undershot is a serious fault. *The lips* are darkly pigmented and are pendulous, falling squarely in front and, toward the back, in loose hanging flews. *The dewlap* is very pronounced. *The neck* is powerful, of good length, and well arched. *The eyes* are soft, sad, and slightly sunken, showing a prominent haw, and in color are brown, dark brown preferred. A somewhat lighter-colored eye conforming to the general coloring of the dog is acceptable but not desirable. Very light or protruding eyes are faults. *The ears* are extremely long, low set, and when drawn forward, fold well over the end of the nose. They are velvety in texture, hanging in loose folds with the ends curling slightly inward. They are set far back on the head at the base of the skull and in repose, appear to be set on the neck. A high set or flat ear is a serious fault.

Forequarters—*The chest* is deep and full with prominent sternum showing clearly in front of the legs. *The shoulders* and elbows are set close against the sides of the chest. The distance from the deepest point of the chest to the ground, while it must be adequate to allow free movement when working in the field, is

Clear, bright eyes are a sign of good health. The Basset's eyes are soft, slightly sunken, and dark in color. *Photo: Marit Jennsen*

not to be more than one-third of the total height at the withers of an adult Basset. The shoulders are well laid back and powerful. Steepness in shoulder, fiddle fronts, and elbows that are out are serious faults. *The forelegs* are short, powerful, and heavy in bone, with wrinkled skin. Knuckling over of the front legs is a disqualification. *The paw* is massive, very heavy with tough heavy pads, well rounded and with both feet inclined equally a trifle outward, balancing the width of the shoulders. Feet that are down at the pastern are a serious fault. *The toes* are neither pinched together nor splayed, with the weight of the forepart of the body borne evenly on each. The dewclaws may be removed.

Body—The rib structure is long, smooth, and extends well back. The ribs are well sprung, allowing adequate room

HEAD
Large and well
proportioned

EYES
Soft and slightly
sunken

EARS
Long, low set, and
drawn forward

NECK
Powerful and of
good length

NOSE
Darkly pigmented,
wide-open nostrils

MUZZLE
Deep and heavy

FOREQUARTERS
Deep and full chest

Ch. Craigwood Higgins of Switchbark, owned
by Jerry and Carol O'Bryant and Baba Monk,
*Winner of Best of Breed, Westminster
Kennel Club, 1996.* Photo: Isabelle Francais

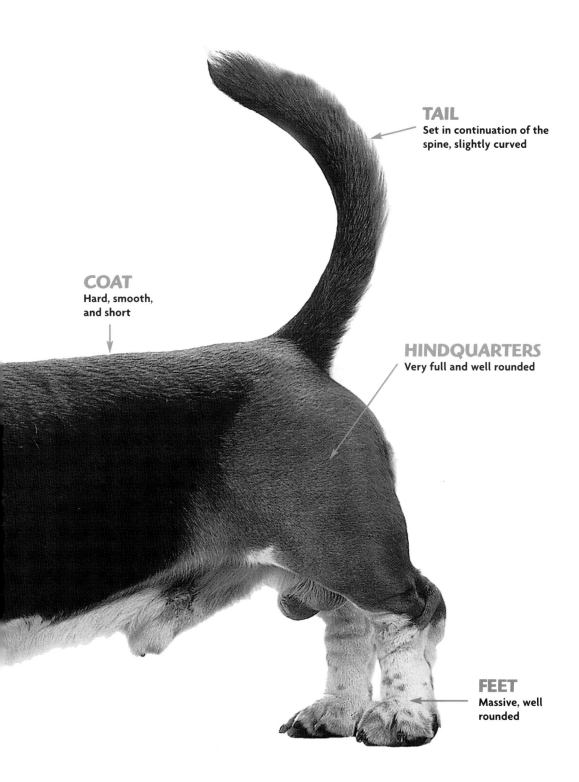

TAIL
Set in continuation of the
spine, slightly curved

COAT
Hard, smooth,
and short

HINDQUARTERS
Very full and well rounded

FEET
Massive, well
rounded

for heart and lungs. Flatsidedness and flanged ribs are faults. The topline is straight, level, and free from any tendency to sag or roach, which are faults.

Hindquarters—The hindquarters are very full and well rounded, and are approximately equal to the shoulders in width. They must not appear slack or light in relations to the over-all depth of the body. The dog stands firmly on its hind legs showing a well-let-down stifle with no tendency toward a crouching stance. Viewed from behind, the hind legs are parallel, with the hocks turning neither in nor out. Cowhocks or bowed legs are serious faults. The hind feet point straight ahead. Steep, poorly angulated hindquarters are a serious fault. The dewclaws, if any, may be removed.

Tail—The tail is not to be docked, and is set in continuation of the spine with but a slight curvature, and carried gaily in hound fashion. The hair on the underside of the tail is coarse.

Size—The height should not exceed 14 inches. Height over 15 inches at the highest point of the shoulder blade is a disqualification.

Gait—The Basset Hound moves in a smooth, powerful, and effortless manner. Being a scenting dog with short legs, it holds its nose low to the ground. Its gait is absolutely true with perfect coordination between the front and hind legs, and it moves in a straight line with hind feet following in line with the front feet, the hocks well bent with no stiffness of action. The front legs do not paddle, weave, or overlap, and the elbows must lie close to the body. Going away, the hind legs are parallel.

Coat—The coat is hard, smooth, and short, with sufficient density to be of use in all weather. The skin is loose and elastic. A distinctly long coat is a disqualification.

Color—Any recognized hound color is acceptable and the distribution of color and markings is of no importance.

DISQUALIFICATIONS

Height of more than 15 inches at the highest point of the shoulder blade.

Knuckled over front legs.

Distinctly long coat.

Approved January 14, 1964

The Basset's long and low set ears are velvety in texture and very useful in the field. This Basset is all ears! *Photo: Evaline Dow*

Bringing Your Basset Hound Home

Before actually collecting your puppy, it will be easier if you purchase the basic items that you will need in advance of the pup's arrival date. Ask the breeder what food the puppy is eating and have a supply on hand before the puppy arrives.

It is always better to collect the puppy as early in the day as possible so that he has a few hours with your family before it is time to retire for his first night's sleep

Take your Basset puppy to the veterinarian for a checkup as soon as possible after acquiring him.
Photo: Isabelle Francais

Riding in the car can be a strange and fearful experience for a puppy. The crate will provide your Basset with a safe place to relax when traveling. *Photo: Isabelle Francais*

away from his former home. Ask the breeder to supply you with a toy or cloth that has been with the puppy's mother and littermates. When placed in the puppy's new sleeping area, the familiar smell can be comforting.

At the time that you collect your puppy, breeders in the US should supply you with the puppy's shot and worming record. It is preferable that the puppy has at least two vaccinations before being placed in a new environment. You should always take your new puppy to a veterinarian for a health check as soon as possible, even if he appears to be healthy. Many breeders provide a health guarantee of 72 hours or so and will take the puppy back and refund the purchase price if he is pronounced unhealthy by a veterinarian.

If such a guarantee is offered, be sure to obtain it in writing.

If the puppy is to be AKC registered, the breeder should supply you with his registration papers and a pedigree at the time you take him home. Some breeders may ask you to sign a contract stipulating such things as the spaying or neutering of your dog, sole or co-ownership, or even the type of care that you will provide for your dog. Read any contract carefully and do not sign it unless you understand it and agree to the terms listed.

When collecting your puppy for the trip home, you should bring a travel crate with you and some paper towels to clean up any unexpected accidents. The crate will provide your pup with a safe place to lie down and rest while traveling in the car. If it is a long trip, the puppy will no doubt need to relieve his bowels, so you will have to make a few stops. Do not let the puppy walk where there may have been a lot of other dogs because he might pick up an infection. Also, if he relieves his bowels at such a time, do not just leave the feces where they were dropped. Doing so has resulted in many public parks and other places actually banning dogs. You can purchase poop-scoops from your pet shop and should have them with you whenever you are taking the dog out where he might relieve himself in a public place.

Your journey home should be made as quickly as possible. If it is a hot day, be sure the car interior is amply supplied with fresh air; however, the puppy should never be subject to a draft. If the journey requires an overnight stop at a motel, be aware that other guests will not appreciate a puppy crying half the night. You must regard the puppy as a baby and comfort him so he does not cry for long periods. The worst thing you can do is to shout at him or smack him. This will scare your puppy and get your relationship off to a bad start.

ON ARRIVING HOME

By the time you arrive home, the puppy may be very tired, in which case he should be taken to his sleeping area and allowed to rest. Children should not be allowed to interfere with the pup when he is sleeping. If the pup is not tired, he can be allowed to investigate his new home, but always under your close supervision. After a short look around, the puppy will no doubt appreciate a light meal and a drink of water. Do not overfeed him at his first meal, because he will be in an excited state and more likely to be sick.

Although it is an obvious temptation, you should not invite friends and neighbors to see the new arrival until he has had at least 48 hours in which to settle down. At the very least, the visitors might introduce some bacteria on their clothing that the puppy is not immune to. This aspect is always a risk when a pup has been moved to a new home, so the fewer people the pup meets before he is fully vaccinated, the better.

DANGERS IN THE HOME

Your home holds many potential dangers for a little mischievous puppy, so you must think about these in advance and be sure he is protected from them.

Fireplaces: All open fires should be protected by a mesh screen guard so that there is no danger of the pup being burned by spitting pieces of coal or wood.

Chewing: Puppies just love chewing on things, so be sure that all electrical appliances are neatly hidden from view

Help make your puppy's arrival as comfortable as possible by providing him with a quiet environment and warm bedding. *Photo: Jim Dow*

Your puppy will miss the comfort of his mother and littermates the first few nights in his new home. Give him a familiar toy or leave a nightlight on to help him make the transition. *Photo: Vickie McMackin*

and are not left plugged in when not in use. Keep poisonous plants and toxic objects out of reach and always have Nylabones® and safe toys available for your puppy at all times.

Doors and Windows: A door would seem to be a fairly innocuous object, yet with a strong draft it could kill or injure a puppy easily if it is slammed shut. If you live in a high-rise building, the pup must be protected from falling. Be sure he cannot get through any railings on your patio, balcony, or deck. When leaving upper-story windows open, be sure that all screens are firmly in place.

Kitchens: While many puppies will be kept in the kitchen, at least while they are toddlers and not able to control their bowel movements, the kitchen is a room full of danger, especially while you are cooking. When cooking, keep the puppy in an exercise pen or crate where he can

see you but is safely out of harm's way.

Washing Machines: Be aware when using washing machines that more than one puppy has clambered in to have a nap and received a wash instead! If the washing machine or clothes dryer door is left open and you leave the room for any reason, be sure to check inside the machine before you close the door and switch it on.

Beyond the dangers already cited, you may be able to think of other ones that are specific to your home, such as steep basement steps. Look around your home and check out all potential problems. You'll be glad you did!

THE FIRST NIGHT

The first few nights a puppy spends away from his mother and littermates are quite traumatic for him. He will feel very lonely, maybe cold, and will certainly miss the heartbeat of his siblings when sleeping. To help overcome his loneliness, place a clock that makes a loud ticking sound next to his bed. This may soothe him, as the clock ticks to a rhythm not dissimilar from a heartbeat. A cuddly toy or an object with the scent of his mother and littermates on it, obtained from the puppy's breeder, may also help during the first few nights. A dim nightlight may provide some comfort to the puppy, because his eyes will not yet be fully able to see in the dark, and he may want to leave his bed for a drink or to relieve himself.

If the pup does whimper in the night, there are two things you should not do. One is to get up and chastise him, because he will not understand why you are shouting at him. The other is to rush to comfort him every time he cries, because he will quickly realize that if he wants you to come running, all he needs to do is to holler loud enough.

By all means, give your puppy some extra attention on his first night, but after this, quickly refrain from doing so. The pup will cry for awhile, but then settle down and go to sleep. Some pups are, of course, worse than others in this respect, so you must use balanced judgment in the matter. Many owners take their pups to bed with them. You should only do this if you intend to let this be a permanent arrangement, otherwise it is hardly fair to the puppy. If you have decided to have two puppies, then they will keep each other company and you will have fewer problems.

HOUSETRAINING

Undoubtedly, the first form of training your puppy will undergo is in respect to his toilet habits. To achieve this, you can use either newspaper or scented housetraining pads, which are available at many pet supply stores. A puppy cannot control his bowels until he is a few months old and not fully until he is an adult. Therefore, you must anticipate his needs and be prepared for a few accidents. The prime times a pup will urinate and defecate are shortly after he wakes up from a nap, shortly after he has eaten, and after he has been playing awhile. He will usually whimper and start sniffing the ground, searching the room for a suitable place. You must quickly pick him up and place him on the newspaper or pad. Hold him in position gently but firmly. He might leave without doing anything on the first one or two occasions, but if you simply repeat the procedure every time you think

Until you can train your Basset to go outside, putting down newspapers where you want him to eliminate will prevent accidents from happening. *Photo: Vickie McMackin*

An exercise pen gives your Basset the opportunity to exercise while still keeping him safely confined. *Photo: Isabelle Francais*

he wants to relieve himself, he will eventually get the message.

When he does defecate as required, give him plenty of praise, telling him what a good puppy he is. The pad or newspaper must, of course, be replaced after each use. Puppies do not like using a dirty toilet any more than you do. The pup's toilet can be placed near the door, and as he gets older, it can be placed outside while the door is open. The pup will then start to use it while he is outdoors. From that time on, it will be easy to get the pup to use a given area of the yard. Many breeders recommend the popular alternative of crate training. Upon bringing the pup home, introduce him to

his crate. It should be placed in a restricted, draft-free area of the home. Put the pup's Nylabone® and favorite toys in the crate, along with a wool blanket or other suitable bedding. As the puppy matures and can control his bowels, his natural cleanliness instincts will discourage him from soiling the place where he sleeps, namely his crate. A crate that is approximately two-and-one-half feet long by two feet high is the size that will be needed for an adult Basset. A puppy can use a smaller crate, but make sure to adjust the size of the crate as he grows. The dog should be able to stand and turn around comfortably in his crate. Whenever the pup is taken out of his crate, he should be brought outside (or to his newspaper or pad) to do his business. Never use the crate as a place of punishment. You will see how quickly your pup takes to his crate, considering it his own safe haven from the big world around him.

Do not leave your Basset Hound in his crate for extended periods of time during the day. The crate should be used mainly for sleeping. Ideally, the puppy should be allowed to go in and out of the open crate during the day. If you work all day and are considering leaving your puppy in his crate while you are gone—don't. Other arrangements should be made, because it is not fair to the poor puppy to leave him crated night and day. One solution might be to purchase a tall exercise pen, which will confine the puppy while allowing him room to walk around.

You will, no doubt, be given much advice on how to bring up your puppy. There is no one way that is superior to all others, just as there is no one dog that is an exact replica of another. Each is an individual and must be regarded as such. A dog never becomes disobedient, unruly, or a menace to society without the full consent of his owner. Your puppy may have many limitations, but in so many instances, the single biggest limitation he is confronted with is his owner's inability to understand his needs and how to cope with them.

IDENTIFICATION

It is a sad reflection on our society that the number of dogs that are lost or stolen each year runs into many thousands. You should see that your pet is carrying a permanent identification number, as well as an identification tag on his collar.

Permanent markings come in the form of a tattoo placed on the inner side of a pup's upper rear leg or inside the ear. The number is then recorded with one of the national registration companies. Research laboratories will not purchase dogs carrying numbers, because they realize that these are clearly someone's pet and not abandoned animals. As a result, thieves will normally abandon dogs that are marked, and this, at least, gives the dog a chance to be taken to the dog pound where the number can usually be traced and the dog reunited with his family.

Another permanent form of identification is the microchip. A computer chip that is no bigger than a grain of rice is injected between the dog's shoulder blades. The dog feels no discomfort. He also receives a tag that says he is microchipped. If the dog is lost and picked up by the humane society, they can trace the owner by scanning the microchip. Microchips are usually highly reliable; however, humane societies have reported that they have occasionally migrated from the point of injection. This can make the microchip harder to locate when scanning.

Although a permanent form of identification is strongly recommended, it is also important that your dog always wears a collar and tag along with any other form of identification. A tag takes the form of a metal or plastic disk large enough for you to place the dog's name, your phone number, and possibly your address on it.

In virtually all places in the US, you will be required to obtain a license for your puppy. Laws differ within a state, county, or country, so check with your veterinarian if the breeder has not already advised you on this.

In many cities in the US, a phone system and website are available to aid in the recovery of lost pets. If someone has lost or found a pet, they can call 1-888-pets911 or access a website at www.1888pets911.org. The information that they enter about the lost pet will be immediately added into the local system, and the pet can quickly be reunited with its owner. This service also provides information on animal clinics, adoption, health care, and licenses.

Living with a Basset Hound

A Basset Hound puppy is one of the most irresistible breeds of dog. With a head that seems almost too big for his low body, soft floppy ears, and happy-go-lucky attitude, many people are ready to take home their first Basset Hound puppy on impulse, before becoming familiar with the needs and demands of the breed. This can lead to trouble, because although the Basset can be an easy breed to live with, he does possess certain habits that will not fit in with every owner's lifestyle.

LEARNING TRUST

Basset Hounds were bred to hunt in a pack, and as such they get along well with other dogs and pets. Although your puppy enjoys the company of other dogs, he will crave and actively seek your attention. Playtime with his owner is an important part of the puppy's routine. It helps to develop a special bond of love and trust between owner and hound that will become invaluable when obedience training the independent-minded Basset.

One of the first lessons that your Basset puppy will need to learn is that you are loving yet consistent, firm, and in control. A puppy is like a sponge, soaking up information about the world around him. The first few months of your puppy's life

Being pack dogs, Bassets enjoy the company of one another. However, they also enjoy spending quality time with their owner. *Photo: Evaline Dow*

Bassets have a playful, jovial attitude, which makes playtime that much more fun.
Photo: Brian and Janice Pechtold

PLAYTIME

If you have two puppies, they will naturally keep each other company. However, be sure to give each puppy individual time and attention and teach them good habits. A young pup's day consists primarily of eating, sleeping, and playtime. Almost from the time they can walk, puppies will grab each other's ears and legs and wrestle. They consider this great fun and the game will usually continue until one pup cries, quite vocally, that he has had enough.

A fun game that you can play with your puppy is fetch. Show your pup a ball or a soft toy and throw it a short distance. Your puppy sees the toy as moving prey, and his intention will be to pounce on and capture it. Don't expect your puppy to bring it back to you right away. With gentle coaxing from you, your puppy will soon

will determine how he sees the world—as a warm, inviting place or a cold, insecure place. If a puppy is nurtured with lots of love, attention, and guidance, he will then see his owner as a person to trust and depend on.

Bassets typically have a loving, laid-back disposition, which is especially beneficial in a household with children. This is Kristina and her pal Mona, owned by Claudia Lane and Vickie McMackin.
Photo: Vickie McMackin

realize your part in the game and will readily return the toy for another chance to chase after it. Bassets do not need a lot of exercise, but it is important that you continue to play with your Basset and take him for slow paced, daily walks to keep him exercised and at the proper weight. Many health problems, especially back problems, can be avoided just by keeping your Basset in good physical condition.

FAMILY COMPANION

Bassets love nothing more than to be a part of the family. They are very good with children and love to receive attention. After playtime in the yard, they enjoy curling up in a comfortable dog bed by the sofa. The Basset, typically, has a laid-back disposition. If you are looking for an active dog with the personality of a Golden Retriever, the Basset Hound will not fit the bill. He has a loving, loyal disposition, but the independent Basset will, at times, choose not to be active. At those times, there often is not much that

Bassets have a tendency to drool—everywhere. Provide your pet with his own comfortable bed to prevent him from drooling on your furniture.
Photo: Brian and Janice Pechtold

you can do to change his mind.

Bassets will follow their nose wherever a good scent leads them, so be sure to teach children to keep doors and gates firmly shut, especially if you have a pond or pool. Bassets do not swim well and can easily drown.

AS A WATCHDOG

The Basset Hound is not typically an aggressive breed and will not usually show aggression toward strangers. He will, however, warn you of a stranger's presence with a deep, bellowing bark. At times, he can be quite vocal, so for your neighbors' sake, it is better not to leave him alone in the yard. After sniffing a stranger that you have invited into your home, the Basset will usually return to what he was doing. New dogs are readily welcomed into the household as well.

FUSSY HOUSEKEEPERS BEWARE

A little extra housecleaning is unavoidable if you own a Basset, but there are a few things that you can do that will help. Dinnertime can be messy, because the Basset's long ears can fall in his food and water bowl. Be sure to keep a placemat under his feeding bowls and purchase bowls that are taller and narrower at the opening and specifically designed for a breed with long ears.

Drooling is part of living with a Basset Hound. Their long, droopy flews make them prone to this, so if you don't want drool on your furniture, make sure your hound has his own comfortable bed.

As your Basset matures, his needs will change. Help him stay comfortable and healthy by providing him with good veterinary care, a proper diet, and a lot of love. *Photo: Brian and Janice Pechtold*

Bassets do shed, so regular grooming is required to keep loose hair under control.

CLIMATE CONCERNS

It is important to ensure that your dog remains comfortable and safe in any climate extremes. In warm weather, your Basset should always have plenty of fresh water and shade available to him. Constant panting is a warning sign that your Basset is too hot and should be immediately moved inside to a cooler location. Likewise, the Basset should not be left outside for long periods of time in very cold weather. Even if you buy a dog sweater to keep your hound warm, it will simply not be enough protection in extreme cold.

ADOPTING A BASSET HOUND

Bassets will readily adapt to new surroundings. They naturally enjoy human companionship and will, with time, lovingly bond to a new owner. A national registry such as the American Kennel Club can provide you with the names and phone numbers of persons to contact concerning the adoption or rescue of a Basset Hound.

THE OLDER DOG

Sometime around eight years of age or so, your Basset will start to show his age and his needs will begin to change. He will still enjoy playing with you or his canine companions, but he will tire more easily and need more rest. It is important to make sure that your hound has comfortable bedding in which to sleep. Equally important is that your less active hound maintains the proper weight, which may mean giving him a food specifically designed for an older dog.

Have your older Basset checked by your veterinarian yearly to help him stay healthy. If your vet discovers and treats age-related problem early, it may lead to a longer, more comfortable life for your pet.

Feeding Your Basset Hound

Today's dog owners are fortunate in that they live in an age when considerable cash has been invested in the study of canine nutritional requirements. This means that dog food manufacturers are very concerned about ensuring that their foods are of the best quality. The result

Your Basset's activity level will dictate how much food he needs. Slowmotion's Star Attraction, owned and photographed by Marit Jenssen.

of all their studies, apart from the food itself, is that dog owners are bombarded with advertisements telling them why they must purchase a given brand. The number of products available to you is unlimited, so it is hardly surprising to find that dogs, in general, suffer from obesity and an excess of vitamins rather than the reverse. Be sure to feed age-appropriate food designed to meet the nutritional needs of your puppy, adult, or senior dog. Generally, breeders recommend dry food supplemented by canned if needed.

FACTORS AFFECTING NUTRITIONAL NEEDS

Activity Level: A dog that lives in a country environment and is able to exercise for long periods of the day will need more food than the same breed of dog living in an apartment and given little exercise.

Your Basset will do his best to let you know if he is getting the right amount of food. For example, if he quickly devours his meal, then you are not feeding him enough. *Photo: Isabelle Francais*

Quality of the Food: Obviously, the quality of the food will affect the quantity required by a puppy. If the nutritional content of a food is low, the puppy will need more of it than if a better quality food was fed.

Balance of Nutrients and Vitamins: The average person is not able to combine ingredients to make a dog food that contains the right balance of nutrients and vitamins. Prepared foods are the safest choice.

Genetic and Biological Variation: Apart from all of the other considerations, it should be remembered that each puppy is an individual. His genetic makeup will influence not only his physical characteristics, but also his metabolic efficiency. This being so, two pups from the same litter can vary quite a bit in the amount of food they need to perform the same function under the same conditions. If you consider the potential combinations of all of these factors, you will see that pups of a given breed could vary quite a bit in the amount of food they will require.

AMOUNT TO FEED

The best way to determine dietary requirements is by observing the puppy's general health and physical appearance. If he is well covered with flesh, shows good bone development and muscle, and is an active, alert puppy, then his diet is fine. A puppy will consume about twice as much as an adult of the same breed. You should ask your puppy's breeder to show you the amounts fed to their pups, as this will be a good starting point.

The puppy should eat his meal in about five to seven minutes. Any leftover food can be discarded or placed into the

It is very important to keep your Basset's weight at a normal level. Obesity is one of the leading causes of back problems in the breed. *Photo: Isabelle Francais*

refrigerator until the next meal. Be sure it is fully thawed if your fridge is very cold. Some puppies prefer to have their food slightly warmed.

When serving dry food, make sure that the pieces are small enough so that a young puppy with a tender mouth can chew them. With a young pup, it is preferable to moisten dry food with a little water and mix in a teaspoon or so of canned food. Puppies get excited over the scent of meat and this encourages them to make the transition from mother's milk to commercially prepared dry food.

If the puppy quickly devours his meal and is clearly still hungry, then you are not giving him enough food. If he eats readily but then begins to pick at it or walks away leaving a quantity, then you are probably giving him too much food. Adjust this at the next meal and you will quickly begin to recognize what the correct amount is. If over a number of weeks the pup starts to look fat, then he is obviously overeating; the reverse is true if he starts to look thin. It is extremely important to keep Basset Hounds at a proper weight. Obesity is one of the leading causes of back problems in the breed. Excess weight in the stomach and loin areas pull down on the spine and make it sag, causing problems. Do not add large amounts of human food to your dog's diet. Many of these foods are high in calories. The result will be a spoiled hound on an unbalanced diet.

WHEN TO FEED

It really does not matter what times of the day your puppy is fed, as long as he receives the needed quantity of food. Fresh water should be available throughout the day. Puppies from weaning age to 12 or 16 weeks of age need 3 or 4 meals a day. Older puppies and adult dogs should be fed twice a day. What is most important is that the feeding times are reasonably regular. They can be tailored to fit in with your own timetable, for example, 7 am and 6 pm. The dog will then expect his meals at these times each day. Keeping regular feeding times and feeding set amounts of food will help you to monitor your puppy's or dog's health. If a dog that's normally enthusiastic about mealtimes and eats readily suddenly shows a lack of interest in food, you'll know something is not right.

Lady Di, owned by Jim and Evaline Dow, is a good example of a Basset that is the proper weight and in beautiful condition. *Photo: Evaline Dow*

Grooming Your Basset Hound

The Basset has a hard, short coat that is easy to wash, brush, and dry. Regular brushing, an occasional bath, and other minor grooming will be necessary to keep your hound clean and healthy. The main concerns in grooming the Basset are keeping the coat and skin clean, keeping the ears free from dirt and debris, and trimming the nails.

CLEANING THE SKIN AND COAT

Puppies may be afraid of the feel and sound of running water the first couple of times that they are bathed. To make these

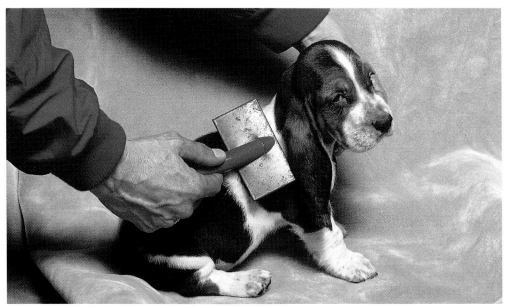

The Basset doesn't require much grooming. Regular brushing and an occasional bath will help keep his coat in good condition. *Photo: Isabelle Francais*

Bassets do tend to shed. Brushing your Basset's coat twice a week will remove loose hairs and keep shedding to a minimum. *Photo: Marit Jenssen*

first, impressionable baths a positive experience, follow a few basic steps.

Always bathe your puppy in a warm place and use warm—never hot or cold—water. Place a nylon collar on him so that you have something other than a wet, squirmy puppy to hold on to, and place him in the tub where he is to be bathed. Have a bucket of warm water available nearby. Dip a washcloth into the bucket and use it to slowly wet your puppy, starting with the feet and working upward. Do the head last. Squeeze some mild dog shampoo onto your hands and gently massage it all over the puppy. He should enjoy his shampoo massage. To keep the puppy from shaking and thus spraying water and shampoo all over, gently hold his muzzle when he starts to shake. Talk to him and tell him what a good puppy he is. Be sure to carefully

avoid his eyes and nose as this would be most uncomfortable for the poor puppy and would surely implant a negative association with bathtime in his mind. If the puppy is especially squirmy, you may want to avoid applying shampoo to the head area altogether.

After your puppy's shampoo is complete, place some warm water into a nonbreakable cup and carefully pour the water over him until he is thoroughly rinsed. Any shampoo residue left in the coat may irritate the skin, so be sure to remove all traces of shampoo. If your puppy does not like the feel of water being poured over his face (and you certainly do not want to get water in his ears), use a wet rag to remove all traces of shampoo from his head.

Thoroughly dry your puppy with a towel. If it is cold and if your puppy will tolerate it, you might finish drying him

It's important that the Basset's ears remain free from debris, which could cause infection. These Bassets are wearing snoods, which keep their ears clean and out of their food bowls. *Photo: Jim Dow*

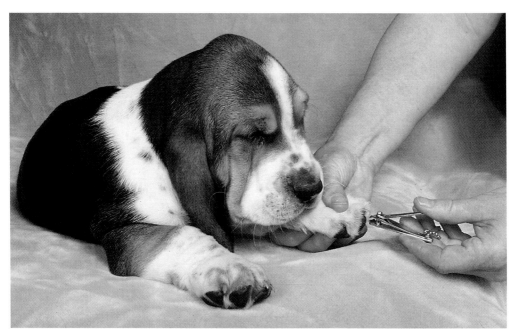

Nail trimming can be uncomfortable for a small puppy. Begin grooming your Basset as soon as possible to familiarize him with the process. *Photo: Isabelle Francais*

with a blow dryer set on low, being careful that the air is not too hot for his tender skin. If it is a warm day, you may want to wash your puppy outside and let him air dry. Once dry, brush your puppy's coat with a soft, natural bristle brush or a hound glove, which can be purchased at a pet supply store. Bassets do tend to shed. To maintain his coat, a thorough, twice-a-week brushing should be enough to remove most loose hairs. If you follow this schedule, you will keep your hound's shedding to a minimum.

EAR CARE

It is important that the ears remain free from debris that might cause infection. Every time you brush your Basset Hound, check his ears for any accumulation of dirt, wax, odor, or redness—any of which would signal the need for attention. The

Basset's long, hanging ears can easily pick up dirt from the ground or harbor moisture inside, so be sure to pay special attention to this area.

To clean your Basset's ears, dampen a cotton ball with a mild soap and water solution. Gently swab only the visible part of the inner side of the ear flap. Never prod deeply into the ear; to do so may cause damage. A cotton swab can be used to aid in the removal of dirt and debris from areas that are visible. Always be gentle, because the inside of the ear flap is sensitive and will bleed easily. The Basset is prone to ear infections, so ask your vet about using a medicated ear wash weekly as a preventative.

NAIL TRIMMING

The most difficult part of nail trimming will be keeping your puppy still. It is

Keeping your pet well groomed is important to his health and well-being. Ch. Bay Manor's Sir Socrates, owned by Jim and Evaline Dow.

always advantageous to have someone helping you the first few times you trim your puppy's nails. The puppy may be as good as gold during the first nail trimming session, only to balk wholeheartedly the next time.

Most nail trimmers sold at pet supply stores will work on a puppy, but when he is grown, be sure to buy a nail trimmer that will easily go through the nails of an adult dog. With an assistant holding the puppy, have him sit. Lift one paw and hold it firmly yet gently in your hand. Be prepared for your puppy to pull his paw back once he realizes what is going on. Before you begin to cut the nail, find the quick (the pink part of the nail that grows from the base and carries the blood supply). Clip just past the quick and by all means do not cut into it, because it will bleed and cause the puppy pain. Always have some styptic powder (which can be purchased from a pet supply store) on hand to stop the bleeding in case you happen to cut into the quick by mistake. If in doubt about how close to the quick to cut, leave more rather than less nail.

How often the nails will need trimming will depend on many factors: genetics, the type of flooring the dog is on, how much of the nail is removed when trimmed, etc. With a young puppy, it is wise to go through the nail trimming routine weekly, even if you do not actually remove any part of the nail, so that the pup becomes accustomed to this procedure. Trimming the nails of an unruly adult can be very difficult.

The Basset Hound is a low-maintenance breed. Basic grooming is all that he requires to look attractive and healthy. *Photo: Isabelle Francais*

Training Your Basset Hound

Once your puppy has settled into your house and responds to his name, you can begin his basic training. Before giving advice on how you should go about doing this, two important points should be made. You should train the puppy in isolation of any potential distractions, and you should keep all lessons very short. It is essential that you have the full attention of your puppy. This is not possible if there are other people about, or the television or radio is on, or other pets are in the vicinity. Even when the pup has become a young adult, the maximum

For the best results, train your puppy in a quiet, relaxing environment that is free of distractions.
Photo: Evaline Dow

Keep training lessons short and fun and remember to end each session with praise and a reward. This will keep your Basset interested and eager to learn. *Photo: Isabelle Francais*

time you should allocate to a lesson is about 20 minutes. However, you can give the puppy more than one lesson a day, three being as many as are recommended, each well spaced apart.

Before beginning a lesson, always play a game with the puppy so he is in an active state of mind and thus more receptive to the matter at hand. The Basset Hound is an independent thinker that will not always enjoy being told what to do. You must make obedience training fun for your hound. Always try to end a lesson with fun time for the pup and on a high note, praising him for something that he has done properly. The exception to this would be if you feel that either you or your hound are reaching the point of frustration. Then it is best to stop the lesson and begin again on another day.

Something that may greatly ease training is the use of food as a reward. Some Basset Hounds will quickly learn to associate the reward with their correct response to your commands. Other Bassets will quickly tire of training and stubbornly refuse to respond. For these hounds, try to keep the lessons fun and exciting by using other means. It may take a lot of time and effort before your Basset will do as you ask. Don't give up. It takes consistency and patience to train a Basset Hound.

COLLAR AND LEASH TRAINING

Training a puppy to his collar and leash is very easy. Place a collar on the puppy. Although he will initially try to bite at it, he will soon forget it, even more so if you play with him. You can leave the collar on

GUIDE TO OWNING A BASSET HOUND

Training your Basset to walk on a leash will give you the chance to enjoy quality time outside together. *Photo: Isabelle Francais*

for a few hours. Some people leave their dog's collar and an identification tag on all of the time. This is a good idea—just be sure that you remove the collar when your pup is not supervised, as accidents can happen all too easily. If the collar is to be left on, purchase a round or narrow one so it does not mark the fur.

Once the puppy ignores the collar, you can attach the leash to it and let the puppy pull it along behind him for a few minutes. However, if the pup starts to chew at the leash, simply hold it, but keep it slack and let the pup go where he wants. The idea is to let him get the feel of the leash, but not get in the habit of chewing it. Repeat this a couple of times a day for two days. The pup will soon get used to the leash without thinking that it will restrain him, which you will not have attempted to do yet.

Next, let the pup understand that the leash will restrict his movements. The first time he realizes this, he will pull and buck or just sit down. Immediately call the pup to you and make a fuss over him. Never tug

A leash and collar allows the dog owner to restrain his dog when necessary. *Photo: Isabelle Francais*

on the leash so the puppy is dragged along the floor, because this simply implants a negative thought in his mind.

If your puppy is particularly stubborn about walking on a leash, hold a small piece of a favorite food treat just out of his reach and let him walk to it. Give him a little bite and repeat this in short training sessions. Soon your puppy will be walking on a leash without these special aids.

THE COME COMMAND

Come is the most vital of all commands. For safety's sake, your hound must learn to reliably come at your command.

To teach the puppy to come, let him reach the end of a long lead, then give the command and say his name, gently pulling him toward you at the same time. As soon as he associates the word "come" with the action of moving toward you, pull only when he does not respond

Once your Basset can sit properly, teach him how to remain in position until you release him.
Photo: Claudia Lane

immediately. As he starts to come, move back to make him learn that he must also come to you from a distance. Soon you may be able to practice without a leash, but if your puppy is slow to come or notably disobedient, go to him and gently pull him toward you, repeating the command. Never scold a dog during this exercise or any other exercise. Remember, the trick is that the puppy must want to come to you. Lavish your dog with praise each time he comes when called. A dog will reliably come when called only if he is taught that no matter what he may have done, if he comes to you when called, he will be praised. For the independent Basset Hound, it is wise to reinforce this lesson by offering a treat each time he comes to you when you call him.

THE SIT COMMAND

You can give the puppy two lessons a day on the sit command, but he will make just as much progress with one 15-minute lesson each day. Some trainers will advise you that you should not proceed to other commands until the previous one has been learned quite well. However, a bright, young pup is quite capable of handling more than one command per lesson and certainly per day. Indeed, as time passes you will be going through each command as a matter of routine before a new one is attempted. This is so the puppy always starts as well as ends a lesson on a high note, having successfully completed something.

Young puppies may have difficulty sitting for a long time. If your Basset seems to be bored, release him and offer him lots of praise.
Photo: Isabelle Francais

Call the puppy to you and praise him. Place one hand on his hindquarters and the other under his upper chest. Say, "Sit" in a pleasant (never harsh) voice. At the same time, gently push down on his rear end and push up under his chest. Once the puppy is in the sit position, release your hands. At first, he will tend to get up, so immediately repeat the exercise. The lesson will end when the pup is in the sit position. Now lavish praise on the puppy and give him a treat. When the puppy understands the command and does it right away, you can slowly move backward so that you are a few feet away from him. If he attempts to come to you, simply place him back in the original position and start again. Do not attempt to keep the pup in the sit position for too long. At this age, even a few seconds is a long while, and you do not want him to get bored with lessons before he has even started them.

THE HEEL COMMAND

All dogs should be able to walk nicely on a leash without their owners being involved in a tug-of-war with them. The heel command will follow leash training. Heel training is best done in an area where you will have a wall to one side of you. This restricts the puppy's lateral movements so that you only have to contend with forward and backward situations. A fence is an alternative, or you can do the lesson in the garage. Again, it is better to do the lesson in private, not on a public sidewalk where there may be many distractions.

With a young puppy, there will be no need to use a choke collar, because you can be just as effective with a regular

Your Basset needs to understand the heel command if you plan to enter him in show competitions. *Photo: Jim Dow*

Give your Basset time to get used to the feel of a leash and collar. Once he feels comfortable, you can go anywhere together without the worry of him wandering off. *Photo: Vickie McMackin*

one. The leash should be of good length, certainly not too short. You can adjust the space between you, the puppy, and the wall, so that your pet has only a small amount of room to move sideways. This being so, he will either hang back or pull ahead; the latter is the more desirable position.

With the puppy on your left side, hold the leash in your right hand and pass it through to your left. As the puppy moves ahead or behind you, give the leash a quick jerk with your left hand, at the same time saying, "Heel." Be sure not to be too harsh. The jerk should get your pup's attention, but not hurt him. The position you want the pup to be in is such that his chest is level with, or just behind, an imaginary line from your knee. When the

puppy is in this position, praise him, give him a treat, and begin walking again. Repeat the whole exercise. Once the puppy begins to get the message, you can use your left hand to pat the side of your leg, which will show him where you want him to be walking.

It is useful to suddenly do an about-turn when the pup understands the basics. He will now be behind you, so you can pat your leg and say, "Heel." As soon as the pup is in the correct position, give him lots of praise and a treat. The puppy will now begin to associate certain words with certain actions. Whenever he is not in the heel position, he will experience displeasure as you jerk the leash, but when he comes alongside you he will receive praise. Given these two options, he will always prefer the latter, assuming that he has no other reason to fear you.

If you have no wall to walk against, things may be a little more difficult because the pup will tend to wander to his left. This means you need to give lateral jerks as well as bring the pup to your side. End the lesson when your Basset puppy is walking nicely beside you. Begin the lesson with a few sit commands, which he understands by now, so that you're starting with success and praise. If your puppy is nervous on the leash, you should never drag him to your side as you may see so many other people do. If the pup sits down, call him to your side and give him lots of praise. He must always come to you because he wants to. If he is dragged to your side, he will see you doing the dragging—a big negative. When he races ahead, he does not see you jerk the leash. In this way, all he knows is that something restricted his movement, and once he was in a given position, you gave him lots of praise. This is using canine psychology to your advantage. Always try to remember that if a dog must be disciplined, try not to let him associate the discipline with you. This is not possible in all matters, but where it is, it is definitely preferred. Some Bassets will simply quit working if given too many corrections, so be wary.

THE STAY COMMAND

The stay command follows from the sit. Face the puppy and say, "Sit." Now step backward, and as you do, say, "Stay." Let the pup remain in the position for only a few seconds before calling him to you and

Puppies are very curious and energetic, which makes staying in one position difficult. Gently help your puppy into position if he is having trouble. *Photo: Isabelle Francais*

The down command can be difficult for dogs to master because it puts them in a submissive position.
Photo: Vickie McMackin

giving him lots of praise. Repeat this, but step farther back. Speak just loudly enough for the pup to hear, yet use a firm voice. You can stretch the word to form a "Sta-a-a-y." If the pup gets up and comes to you, simply lift him up, place him back in the original position, and start again. As the pup comes to understand the command, you can move farther and farther back.

The next test is to walk away after placing the pup in position. This will mean that your back is to him, which will tempt him to follow you. Keep an eye on him over your shoulder and the minute the pup starts to move, turn around and in a more stern voice, say either "Sit" or "Stay." If the pup has gotten quite close to you, return him to the original position.

As the weeks go by, you can increase the length of time the pup is left in the stay position, but two to three minutes is quite long enough for a puppy. If your puppy drops into a lying position and is clearly more comfortable, there is nothing wrong with this. Likewise, your pup will want to face the direction in which you walked off. Some trainers will prefer that the dog face the direction he was placed in, regardless of whether or not you move off on his blind side.

THE DOWN COMMAND

From the puppy's viewpoint, the down command can be one of the more difficult ones to accept. This is because the down position is one taken by a submissive dog in a wild pack situation. A timid dog will roll over, which is a natural gesture of submission. A bolder pup will want to get up and may back off, not feeling he should have to submit to this command. He will feel that he is under attack from you and about to be punished, which is what the position would be in his natural environment. Once he understands that this is not the case, he will accept the unnatural position.

Stand in front of the pup and tell him to sit. Now kneel down, which is immediately far less intimidating to the puppy than having you tower above him. Take each of his front legs and pull them forward, at the same time saying, "Down." Release the legs and quickly apply light pressure on the shoulders with your left hand. Then, just as quickly, say, "Good boy" and give your puppy lots of praise. Offer a treat as a reward. Repeat two or three times only. Remember, this is a very submissive act on the pup's behalf, so there is no need to rush matters.

RECALL TO HEEL COMMAND

When your puppy is coming to the heel position from an off-leash situation—for example, when he has been running free—

he should do so in the correct manner. He should pass behind you, take up his position, and then sit. To teach this command, have the pup in front of you in the sit position with his collar and leash on. Hold the leash in your right hand. Give him the command to heel and pat your left knee. As the pup starts to move forward, use your right hand to guide him behind you. If need be, you can hold his collar and walk him around the back of you to the desired position. You will need to repeat this a few times, until he understands what is wanted.

When he has done this a number of times, and you are sure that he will come to you when called, you can try it without the leash. If the pup comes up toward your left side, bring him to the sit position in front of you, hold his collar, and walk him around the back of you. He will eventually understand and automatically pass around your back each

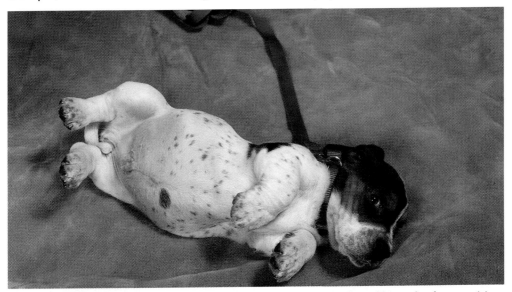

This puppy is just going to keep rolling over until he can maneuver himself into the down position.
Photo: Isabelle Francais

Socialization is an important part of your Basset's development. Learning how to get along with unfamiliar dogs will help him to be comfortable and well behaved in different situations.
Photo: Isabelle Francais

time. If the dog is already behind you when you recall him, then he should automatically come to your left side, which you will be patting with your hand. Always praise your pup and offer a treat for a job well done.

THE NO COMMAND

This is a command that must be obeyed every time without fail. Most delinquent dogs have never been taught this command—included in these are the jumpers, the barkers, and the biters. In the event that your puppy approached a poisonous snake or any other potential danger, the no command, coupled with the recall, could save his life. You do not need to give a specific lesson for this command because it will crop up time and again in day-to-day life.

If the puppy is chewing a slipper, you should approach the pup, take hold of the slipper, and say, "No" in a stern voice. If he jumps onto the furniture and you do not want him to, lift him off, say, "No," and place him gently on the floor. You must be consistent in the use of the command and apply it every time he is doing something you do not want him to do.

Never allow your Basset Hound pup to step out of the front door of your home or out of your car door until you give him the command, "OK." If he does leave without your approval, say, "No" in a stern voice and place him back into the house or car. Dogs are usually excited when they leave home, and this simple step can save your pup from excitedly running onto a busy street full of traffic.

SOCIALIZATION

When your Basset Hound is leash-broken and has had his series of puppy shots, it is important to socialize him. Take him to public places often, such as a park, so that he can become familiar with new sights, sounds, and people. This is an important step in the development of your puppy and will ensure that he is comfortable in many different situations.

Showing Your Basset Hound

Showing your Basset Hound can be a fun and rewarding experience. The Basset is well suited to many forms of competition; however, there are several things to consider before choosing an event to participate in. First, you must decide on your area of interest. Two important factors affecting this decision

Ch. Sanlyn Classic Sportster, owned by Claudia Lane and Vicki McMackin, won Best of Breed over more than 300 Bassets at the 1999 National Basset Hound Club of America Specialty Show. To date, he has won 24 Specialty Bests in Show. *Photo: "Elaine"*

Ch. Beaujangle's J.P. Beaureguarde, owned by Claudia Lane and Vickie McMackin, is shown all the way to Best in Show. *Photo: Kohler*

will probably be time and money. Time is an important element because some events require long hours of training essential for success. Expenses can differ with each event and costs to compete can run from a few dollars to several hundred dollars. Research your area of interest before making an investment. A national registry such as the American Kennel Club can provide you with a listing of clubs to contact in your chosen field of interest.

CONFORMATION SHOWS

In conformation showing, your Basset will be competing against other Basset Hounds, all of which are compared to the breed's standard of excellence by a judge. The breed standard gives a detailed description of the correct conformation, movement, and qualities of the Basset Hound and is adopted by the kennel club that your dog is registered with, such as the American Kennel Club in the US and The Kennel Club in England. The judge examines each dog and chooses his or her winners based on how well the dogs conform to the breed standard. One dog from each breed is chosen for further competition against dogs of other breeds.

The manner in which your Basset is presented to the judge can make a considerable difference in both your dog's appearance and the judge's impression of him. The best place to start is at a handling class. These classes are usually held once a week. There, you and your dog will be with other owners and

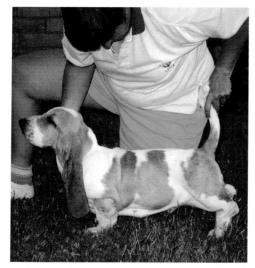

Make sure that your Basset adheres to the breed standard before entering him in conformation showing. *Photo: Evaline Dow*

instructing you on how to move your dog around the ring. Your Basset will become accustomed to unfamiliar surroundings, dogs, people, and actual ring procedure. The instructor will give you tips on how to properly present your hound in the ring.

Not every dog will possess all of the qualities necessary to become a champion show dog. If you wish to pursue conformation showing, have your Basset's breeder evaluate your dog when he is grown. If his attributes do not fall into the conformation show dog category, don't worry. He will probably excel in other areas. Always remember that whether a show dog or a pet, every dog deserves a great home with lots of love.

their dogs in a situation very similar to a real dog show. An instructor will act as the judge, examining your dog and

Ch. Blue Belle's Red Rufus CGC taking the ribbon, owned by Brian and Janice Pechtold. *Photo: Robert Skibinski*

OBEDIENCE

Obedience is an event in which your dog is judged and awarded points based on how well he performs set exercises according to your directions. There are several levels of achievement that are offered in obedience, and your dog will earn titles when he completes the requirements for each level. Many years of training are usually required to earn the higher titles of achievement.

Food rewards play an important role in training the Basset Hound, as most are not anxious to follow your directions and require motivation. Find an obedience trainer who understands the stubborn nature of the Basset and is willing to use food, praise, and whatever method that may work, rather than harsh corrections. Obedience classes are readily available in almost all areas and are an invaluable aid in preparing your dog for the ring.

TRACKING

Tracking is a sport in which the Basset Hound's highly developed sense of smell enables him to excel. Your hound will be required to follow a human scent for a set distance. There are a variety of tracking titles that can be earned. The beginning title is for completing the shortest and easiest course. Advanced titles require that the hound follow a longer, obstacle-laden track with an older scent that has been left on various surfaces, making it more difficult to follow. Many clubs hold tracking classes and most offer puppy classes to get the

Tracking enables the Basset to use his highly developed sense of smell. The field Basset is a sound, athletic hound. *Photo: Marit Jenssen*

youngsters excited about the sport and off to a good start.

FIELD TRIALS

Field trials are what the Basset Hound was bred for. These events enable your Basset to display his ability to follow the scent of a live rabbit as it runs, leaving a twisting, turning trail. He is judged on how accurately he stays with the scent of the rabbit. A deep, bellowing bark is required when he picks up a scent, and it serves to notify his owner that he has found the trail. Points are awarded according to placement earned and accumulated toward a championship title. The field Basset is very much an athlete, requiring conditioning, soundness of body, and cleverness in the field.

There are many other events that might be of interest to you and your Basset. Be sure to attend the type of event that sparks your interest. Talk to exhibitors about the sport. They can be of great help in guiding you in the right direction.

Your Healthy Basset Hound

Most Bassets live a long and healthy life, but there are a few problems that may affect your hound and you should be aware of what to watch for.

Dogs, like all other animals, are capable of contracting problems and diseases that, in most cases, are easily avoided by sound husbandry. This means that well-bred and well-cared-for animals are less prone to developing diseases and problems than are carelessly bred and neglected animals. Your knowledge of how to avoid problems is far more valuable than all of the books and advice on how to cure them. The only person you should listen to about treatment is your vet. Veterinarians don't have all the answers, but at least they are trained to analyze and treat illnesses and are aware of the full implications of various treatments. This does not mean that a few old remedies aren't good standbys when all else fails, but in most cases, modern science provides the best treatments for disease. Remember, many problems can be easily treated when caught early. Your puppy should

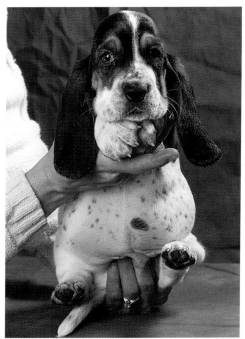

Purchasing your Basset from a reliable, knowledgeable breeder ensures that he is less prone to developing health problems.
Photo: Isabelle Francais

Safe chewing bones help keep your Basset's teeth clean and healthy, while at the same time provide him with entertainment. *Photo: Isabelle Francais*

receive regular veterinary examinations or checkups. At the first sign of a potential problem, always consult your veterinarian as soon as possible.

HEALTHY TEETH AND GUMS

Chewing is instinctual. Puppies chew so that their teeth and jaws grow strong and healthy as they develop. As the permanent teeth begin to emerge, it is painful and annoying to the puppy. Unfortunately, once the puppy's permanent teeth have grown in and settled solidly into the jaw, the chewing instinct does not fade. Adult dogs instinctively need to clean their teeth, massage their gums, and exercise their jaws through chewing.

It is necessary for your dog to have clean teeth. You should take your dog to the veterinarian at least once a year to have his teeth cleaned and to have his mouth examined for any sign of oral disease. Although dogs do not get cavities in the same way humans do, dogs' teeth accumulate tartar more quickly than humans. Veterinarians recommend brushing your dog's teeth daily, but with our busy schedules who can find time to do this on a daily basis? The accumulation of tartar and plaque on our dogs' teeth, when not removed, can cause irritation, eventually erode the enamel, and finally destroy the teeth. Advanced cases, along with destroying the teeth, bring on gingivitis and periodontitis, two very serious conditions that can affect the dog's internal organs as well—to say nothing about bad breath!

Providing the dog with something safe to chew on will help maintain oral hygiene. Chew devices from Nylabone® keep dogs' teeth clean, but they also provide an excellent resource for entertainment and relief of doggie tensions. Your dog will be taking an active part in keeping his teeth and gums healthy without even realizing it.

Nylabone® provides fun bones, challenging bones, and safe bones. It is an owner's responsibility to recognize safe chew toys from dangerous ones. Your dog will chew and devour anything you give him. Dogs must not be permitted to chew on items that they can break. Pieces of broken objects can cause internal damage, besides ripping the dog's mouth. Cheap plastic or rubber toys can cause stoppage in the intestines; such stoppages are operable only if caught immediately.

The most obvious choice of chew toys, in this case, may be the worst choice—natural beef bones. Bones were not designed for chewing and cannot take too much pressure from the sides. Due to the abrasive nature of beef bones, they should be offered most sparingly. If a piece of bone is swallowed, at the very least, digestion is interrupted; at worst, the dog can choke or suffer from intestinal blockage.

When a dog chews hard on a Nylabone®, little bristle-like projections appear on the surface of the bone. These help to clean the dog's teeth and add to the gum massaging. Given the chemistry of the nylon, the bristle can pass through the dog's intestinal tract without effect. Since nylon is inert, no microorganism can grow on it, and it can be washed in soap and water, or sterilized in boiling water or in an autoclave.

For the sake of your dog, his teeth, and your own peace of mind, provide your dog with Nylabones®. They have 100 variations from which to choose.

FIGHTING FLEAS

Fleas are very mobile and may be red, black, or brown in color. The adults suck the blood of the host, while the larvae feed on the feces of the adults, which is rich in blood. Flea "dirt" may be seen on the pup as very tiny clusters of blackish specks that look like freshly ground pepper. The eggs of fleas may be laid on the dog, though they are more commonly laid off the host in a favorable place such as the bedding. They normally hatch in 4 to 21 days, depending on the temperature, but can survive for up to 18 months if temperature conditions are not immediately favorable. The larvae are maggot-like and molt a couple of times before forming pupae, which can survive long periods until the temperature or the vibration of a nearby host causes them to emerge. When they find a host, they jump on and the cycle begins again.

There are a number of effective treatments available. You should discuss them with your veterinarian and follow all instructions for the one you choose. Any treatment will involve a product for your puppy or dog and one for the environment. It will also require diligence on your part to treat all areas and thoroughly clean your home and yard until the infestation is eradicated.

Check your Basset's coat thoroughly for fleas and ticks after he has been playing outside.
Photo: Isabelle Francais

THE TROUBLE WITH TICKS

Ticks are arthropods of the spider family, which means they have eight legs (though the larvae have six). They bury their headparts into the host and gorge on its blood. Ticks are easily seen as small, grain-like creatures sticking out from the skin. They are often picked up when dogs play in fields, but may also arrive in your yard via wild animals such as birds or stray animals such as cats and dogs. The most troublesome type of tick is the deer tick, which spreads the deadly Lyme disease that can cripple a dog (or a person). Deer ticks are tiny and very hard to detect. Often, by the time they're big enough to notice, they've been feeding on the dog for a few days, which is long enough to do damage. Your veterinarian can advise you of the danger to your dog in your area, and may suggest that your dog be vaccinated for Lyme disease. Always go over your Basset with a fine-toothed comb when you come in from walking through any area that may harbor deer ticks. If your dog is acting unusually sluggish or sore, seek veterinary advice.

Attempts to pull a tick free will invariably leave the headpart in the dog, where it will die and cause an infected wound or abscess. The best way to remove ticks is to dab a strong saline solution, iodine, or alcohol on them. This will numb them, causing them to loosen their hold, at which time they can be removed with forceps. The wound can then be cleaned and covered with an antiseptic ointment. If ticks are common

If you are concerned about ticks in your area, your vet can advise you of the danger to your Basset. He may also suggest that your dog be vaccinated for Lyme disease.
Photo: Isabelle Francais

Bassets enjoy time in the great outdoors. Be sure to take every precaution to prevent your Basset from becoming infested with parasites.
Photo: Morten Olsen

in your area, consult with your vet for a suitable pesticide to be used in kennels, on bedding, and on the puppy or dog.

SKIN DISORDERS

Apart from the problems associated with lesions created by biting pests, a dog may develop a number of other skin disorders. Seeds or thorns can get lodged in the fur or between toes and cause an abscess. It is wise to check your dog regularly for these problems.

Other skin disorders may be caused by ringworm, mange, or eczema. Ringworm is not caused by a worm, but is a fungal infection. It manifests itself as a sore-looking, bald circle. If your dog should have any form of bald patches, let your veterinarian check him over. A microscopic examination can confirm the condition. Many old remedies for ringworm exist, such as iodine, carbolic acid, formalin, and other tinctures, but modern drugs are superior.

Fungal infections can be very difficult to treat and even more difficult to eradicate because of the spores, which can withstand most treatments except burning. Bedding should be incinerated or properly discarded once the condition has been confirmed.

Mange is a general term that can be applied to many skin conditions in which the hair falls out and a flaky crust develops and falls away. Often, dogs will scratch themselves and this invariably creates a condition worse than the original one, because it opens lesions that are then subject to viral, fungal, or parasitic attack. The cause of the problem can be various species of mites. These either live on skin debris and the hair follicles, which they destroy, or they bury themselves just beneath the skin and feed on the tissue. Applying general remedies from pet stores is not recommended because it is essential to identify the type of mange before a specific treatment can be effective.

Eczema is another nonspecific term applied to many skin disorders. The condition can be brought about in many ways. Sunburn, chemicals, allergies to foods, drugs, pollens, and even stress can all produce a deterioration of the skin and coat. Given the range of causal factors, it is a case of taking each possibility at a time and trying to correctly diagnose the matter. If the cause is of a dietary nature, you must remove one item at a time in

Check your Basset's paws after he has been playing outside. Seeds or thorns can get wedged in the fur or between his toes and cause a painful abscess. *Photo: Isabelle Francais*

Allergies to foods, drugs, stress, and sunburn are just some of the things that can cause skin problems for your Basset. If a certain condition persists, consult your veterinarian. *Photo: Brian and Janice Pechtold*

order to find out if the dog is allergic to a given food. The problem could be caused by the lack of a nutrient, so if the condition persists you should consult your veterinarian.

INTERNAL DISORDERS

It cannot be overstressed that it is very foolish to attempt to diagnose an internal disorder without the advice of a veterinarian. When you suspect a problem, it's up to your vet to make the correct diagnosis. The following symptoms, especially if they accompany each other or are progressively added to earlier symptoms, indicate that you should visit the veterinarian right away:

Continual vomiting. All dogs vomit from time to time and this is not necessarily a sign of illness. They will eat grass to induce vomiting. It is a natural cleansing process common to many carnivores. However, continued vomiting is a clear sign of a

Always handle a puppy gently; however, if he yelps even when lifted carefully, there might be a problem internally. *Photo: Vickie McMackin*

All dogs need an occasional nap or two in the middle of the day; however, if your Basset is unusually listless, there may be a health problem. *Photo: Evaline Dow*

problem. It may be caused by a blockage in the dog's intestinal tract, it may be induced by worms, or it could be due to any number of diseases.

Diarrhea. This, too, may be nothing more than a temporary condition due to many factors. Even a change of home can induce diarrhea, because it often stresses the dog and invariably changes the diet. If it persists more than 48 hours, something is amiss. If blood is seen in the feces, waste no time at all in taking the dog to the vet.

Running eyes and/or nose. A pup may have a chill, and this will cause the eyes and nose to weep. Again, this should quickly clear up if the puppy is placed in a warm environment and away from any drafts. If it does not, and especially if a mucous discharge is seen, the dog has an illness that must be diagnosed. Some Basset Hounds are prone to eye infections, which can be triggered by allergies to mold, grasses, and other pollens. At the first sign of a problem, contact your vet.

Coughing. Prolonged coughing is a sign of a problem, usually of a respiratory nature.

Wheezing. If the dog has difficulty breathing or makes a wheezing sound when breathing, then something is wrong.

Cries when attempting to defecate or urinate. This might only be a minor problem due to the hard state of the feces, but it could be more serious, especially if the dog cries when urinating.

Cries when touched. Obviously, if you do not handle a puppy with care, he might yelp. However, if he cries even when lifted gently, or the adult dog whimpers when he moves, then he has an internal problem that becomes apparent when pressure is applied to a given area of the body. Clearly, this must be diagnosed.

Refuses food. Generally, puppies and dogs are greedy creatures when it comes to feeding times. Some might be more fussy, but none should refuse more than one meal. If your dog goes for a number of hours without showing any interest in his food, then something is not as it should be.

General listlessness. All dogs have off days when they do not seem their usual cheeky, mischievous selves. If this condition persists for more than two days, there is little doubt of a problem. They may not show any of the signs listed other than perhaps a reduced interest in their food. There are many diseases that can develop internally without displaying obvious signs. Blood, fecal, and other tests are needed in order to identify the disorder before it reaches an advanced state that may not be treatable.

WORMS

There are many species of worms, and a number of these live in the tissues of dogs and most other animals. Many create no problem at all, so you are not even aware they exist. Others can be tolerated in small levels but become a major problem if they number more than a few. The most common types seen in dogs are roundworms and tapeworms. While roundworms are the greater problem, tapeworms require an intermediate host and are therefore more easily eradicated.

Larval worms can migrate to the womb of a pregnant bitch or to her mammary

Worms can be passed from mother to puppy. Puppies should be wormed when they are about two weeks of age. *Photo: Isabelle Francais*

glands, which is how they pass to the puppy. The pregnant bitch can be wormed, which will help. The pups can and should be wormed when they are about two weeks old. Repeat the worming every 10 to 14 days and the parasites should be removed. Worms can be extremely dangerous to young puppies, so you should be sure the pup is wormed as a matter of routine.

Heartworm infestation in dogs is passed by mosquitoes, but can be prevented by a monthly (or daily) treatment that is given orally. Talk to your vet about the risk of heartworm in your area.

VACCINATIONS

Every puppy, purebred or mixed breed, should be vaccinated against the major

Puppies should get their first vaccinations for the major canine diseases at six to eight weeks of age. *Photo: Isabelle Francais*

canine diseases. These are distemper, leptospirosis, hepatitis, coronavirus, and canine parvovirus. Your puppy should have received a temporary vaccination against these diseases before you purchased him, but ask the breeder to be sure. Additionally, there is an intranasal spray available that provides protection against canine cough.

The age at which vaccinations are given can vary, but most Basset Hound breeders give the first puppy shots at around six to eight weeks of age. Antibodies received from the puppy's mother via her milk will decline with the introduction of solid foods. Be sure to consult your veterinarian on the proper timing of your puppy's shots. Immunization is not 100 percent guaranteed to be successful, but is very close.

Your puppy or dog should also be vaccinated against the deadly rabies virus. In fact, in many places it is illegal for your dog not to be vaccinated for this. The vaccination protects your dog, your family, and the rest of the animal population from this deadly virus that infects the nervous system and causes dementia and death. In most places, it must be given by a veterinarian and proof of such will usually be needed to obtain a license for your dog. Check the local ordinances in your area.

Dogs are subject to other viral attacks, and if these are of a high-risk factor in your area, your vet will suggest you have the puppy vaccinated against these as well.

BLEEDING DISORDERS

Canine thrombopathia is caused by a blood platelet defect. Von Willebrand's disease results from a defect with a protein found in the blood. Both of these diseases cause blood coagulation problems, which result in increased bleeding. They can be hereditary in nature; however, some blood coagulation disorders can be triggered by certain medications or other diseases. Signs to watch for include bleeding from the mouth or nose, excessive bleeding from wounds, blood in the urine or feces, or red spots on the underside of the belly. Your veterinarian may recommend testing if these diseases are suspected.

BLOAT (GASTRIC DILATATION)

Bloat has proved to be fatal in many dogs, especially large and deep-chested breeds; however, any dog can get bloat. Bloat is caused by swallowing air during exercise, food/water gulping, or other strenuous tasks. It is not the result of flatulence as many believe. The stomach of the affected dog twists, disallowing food and blood flow and resulting in harmful toxins being released into the bloodstream. Death can easily follow if the condition goes undetected. As the name implies, symptoms may include a bloated look to the dog's stomach area. The dog may also exhibit signs of being uncomfortable.

The best preventative measure is not to feed large meals or exercise your puppy or dog immediately after he has

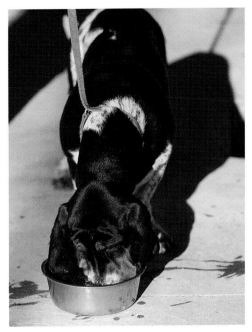

Swallowing air during exercise or eating may cause bloat in dogs, which can be fatal. Watch that your Basset doesn't gulp his water or food too quickly. *Photo: Isabelle Francais*

eaten. When concerned about bloat, veterinarians recommend feeding three smaller meals per day in an elevated feeding rack, adding water to dry food to prevent gulping, and not offering water during mealtimes.

CANCER

Cancer is on the rise in both humans and dogs. It is important to check your Basset regularly for any signs of lumps or changes in the skin. Run you hands slowly and carefully over his body, feeling for any lumps under the skin or any growths that may be on the skin. Don't forget to check between your dog's toes. If you feel a lump, have your vet examine it as soon as possible. Some lumps are nothing to worry about; however, some innocent

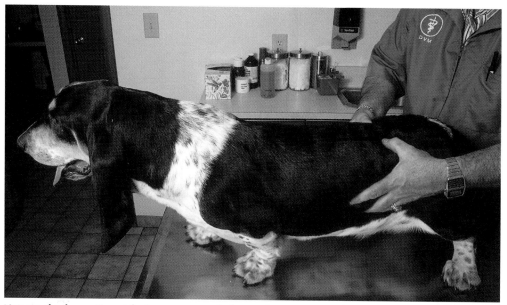
You can check your Basset for lumps or growths by gently running your hands over the length of his body.
Photo: Isabelle Francais

looking lumps may turn cancerous and the sooner these are removed, the less chance that the disease will spread.

Spaying and neutering your pet is the best way to prevent cancers that form in the reproductive system. The best time to have these procedures performed is around six months of age, before your dog becomes sexually mature.

CHERRY EYE

Cherry eye appears as a swollen, red mass, which is often accompanied by drainage. It is caused by the prolapse of the tear gland of the third eyelid. Your vet may recommend surgery for this condition.

EAR DISORDERS

There are many types of bacteria, yeast, or mold that can cause infections in the ear. The Basset's long, droopy ears can sometimes retain constant moisture, which may trigger these infections. Signs can include a brown discharge, odor, or redness. Foreign debris can also lodge deep within the ear canal, causing pain and infection. The dog may scratch at the ear, whimper, and shake his head often. It is important to have your veterinarian diagnose the specific cause of an infection and prescribe a cure. A medication that may work for one type of bacteria might be useless on another. Left untreated, ear infections can lead to serious problems or even death.

EYELID PROBLEMS

Ectropian (when the eyelid turns in) and entropian (when the eyelid turns out) conditions can both cause problems in the Basset Hound. Your veterinarian may recommend surgery to correct these conditions.

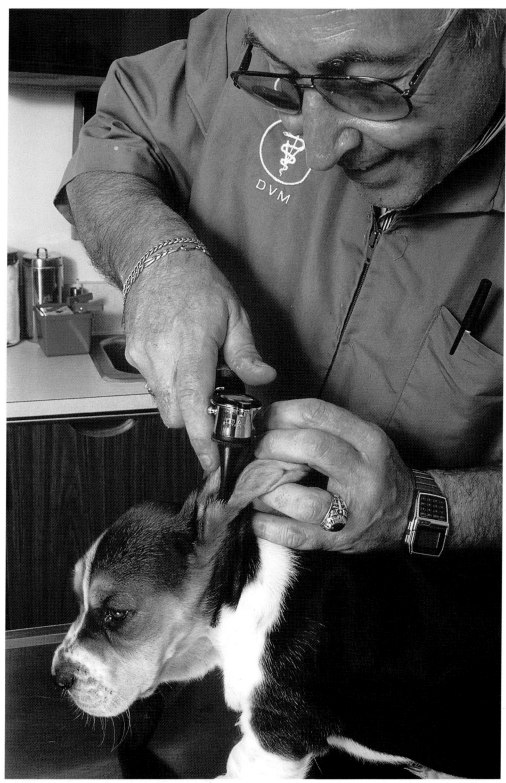

The Basset's long, droopy ears tend to retain constant moisture, which may trigger ear infections. Symptoms include a brown discharge, odor, or redness. *Photo: Isabelle Francais*

Keeping a watchful eye on your Basset will help prevent any accidents from happening.
Photo: Robert Pearcy

GLAUCOMA

Glaucoma is a disease that causes an increase of pressure in the eye that damages the optic nerve and retina. Damage can occur rapidly. In the Basset Hound, glaucoma may be hereditary, but can also be caused by trauma, infection, or other causes. Glaucoma can cause much damage before the problem is noticed, so precautionary veterinary testing is wise.

HYPOTHYROIDISM

Hypothyroidism usually develops as a result of a disease of the thyroid gland. Symptoms can include weight gain, shivering, loss of hair, dry hair, lessened physical activity, or changes in the feces. Medication can help to keep this condition under control. Coal-tar-based shampoos are often used to help alleviate skin symptoms.

INTERVERTEBRAL DISK DISEASE

Intervertebral disk disease causes damage to the spinal cord and/or spinal nerve roots. Pain is usually present and the disease can progress to cause paralysis. Treatment may include rest, medication, or surgery in severe cases. Bassets should be discouraged from jumping on or off furniture, because this can be a cause of injury.

PANOSTEITIS

Panosteitis is a disease that can be difficult to diagnose. It causes lameness in young Basset Hounds. The cause is unknown. Bassets usually outgrow this problem by the age of two years. Medication to treat the painful symptoms is helpful.

SEIZURES

There are many causes of seizures, including vitamin deficiencies, parasites, or intestinal obstructions. Some seizures are thought to be hereditary in nature. These typically consist of reoccurring seizures that begin in the first or second year of life. Seizures can sometimes be controlled with medication.

SPONDYLOSIS

Spondylosis is a progressive, degenerative condition of the disks and vertebrae, occurring more often in the older Basset. Pain may be present as the disease progresses. Medication to treat the symptoms can be prescribed by your veterinarian.

ACCIDENTS

All puppies will get their share of bumps and bruises due to the rather energetic way they play. They will usually heal themselves over a few days. Small cuts should be bathed with a suitable disinfectant and then smeared with an antiseptic ointment. If a cut looks more serious, stem the flow of blood with a towel or makeshift tourniquet and rush the pup to the veterinarian. Never apply so much pressure to the wound that it might restrict the flow of blood to the limb.

In the case of serious burns, apply cold water or an ice pack to the surface. If the burn was due to a chemical, it must be washed away with ample amounts of water. Apply petroleum jelly to the burn. Trim away the hair if need be. Wrap the dog in a blanket and rush him to the vet. The pup may go into shock, depending on the severity of the burn. This may result in a lowered blood pressure, which is dangerous and the reason the pup must receive immediate veterinary attention.

If a broken limb is suspected, then try to keep the animal as still as possible. Wrap your pup or dog in a blanket to restrict movement and get him to the veterinarian as soon as possible. Do not move the dog's head so it is tilting backward, because this may cause blood to enter the lungs.

Do not let your pup jump up and down from heights, because this may cause considerable shock to the joints. Like all youngsters, puppies do not know when enough is enough, so you must do all of their thinking for them.

Provided you apply strict hygiene to all aspects of raising your puppy and you make daily checks on his physical state, you have done as much as you can to safeguard him during his most vulnerable period. Routine visits to your veterinarian are also recommended, especially while the puppy is under one year of age.

Index